fun with
NATURE

LIZ BOMFORD

CONTENTS

Special equipment	2
The conservation patch	4
Pond dipping	6
Frogs and toads	8
Fungi	10
The seashore	12
Keeping marine animals	14
Birdwatching	16
Building for birds	18
Catching insects	20
Trees	22
Mammals	24
Plants	26
The soil	30
Index	32

HAMLYN

SPECIAL EQUIPMENT

"Environment" is a much used word today. This is because all over the world we have come to realize that man does not live alone, but in delicate balance with the wild animals and plants of the natural world. We need to learn about nature for our own survival. Nature is not dull. Things are happening around us all the time. Even if you spent your whole life studying nature you could never hope to know everything, so there is plenty of room for amateur naturalists to make their own studies. Many important discoveries have been found by amateurs.

This book will help you find out how nature works. Not only by reading about it, but by doing really interesting projects.

Most of the basic equipment you will need is cheap and easy to obtain.

A nature table should be strong enough to support the weight of your aquarium and big enough to allow you to sort out the masses of shells and seaweeds, bones and caterpillars that you are bound to collect as you become more and more interested. If you haven't got room for a whole table a nature shelf will do fine, and a piece of soft board on the wall behind will display some of your collection splendidly.

A notebook with a pencil attached should be always in your pocket. This is to jot down casual observations in the field. It's no good trying to remember things when you get home. Try to make a few rough drawings as well. You can keep a proper *Nature diary* on the nature table in which you write up your findings and make more careful illustrations. It's a good idea to use maps and photographs if you can. This adds a really professional touch!

pooter

fixative

Hides or blinds are useful for observation and photography. You can make a simple hide out of greenish brown cotton or canvas stretched over a frame of sticks (see page 17).

A hand lens or magnifying glass is indispensable to real nature watchers. Use one to take a look at the detail of a butterfly's wing or the sting of a nettle or a wasp.

Binoculars are absolutely necessary for birdwatching; 8 × 30 magnification is ideal to start with.

A good torch is invaluable for night-time explorations.

A fishing net for pond dipping can be made with a circle of stiff wire attached to a long pole and covered with netting, or cheap ones are easily available. For catching very small aquatic animals you can attach a plastic container to the bottom of the net.

You will need lots of containers – boxes, small tins, saucers and other containers, in which to carry your discoveries home. Fungi, flowers and feathers are very fragile. Each needs a special travelling box. You will need a plastic bucket with a lid for expeditions to the stream. Try begging one from your local delicatessen or supermarket. And don't forget your rubber boots!

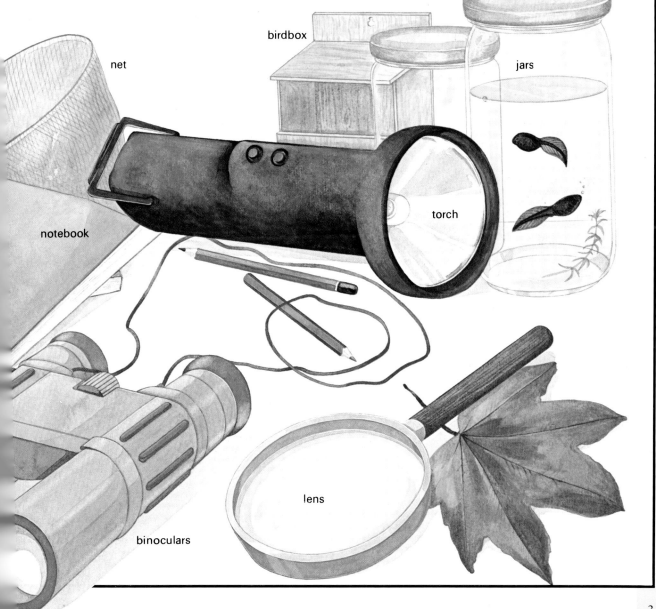

net

birdbox

jars

notebook

torch

lens

binoculars

THE CONSERVATION PATCH

A conservation patch is a good place to study wildlife. A corner of the garden, a piece of rough ground, even a city windowbox can attract wildlife to it. Think of your conservation patch as an animal café and rest area. If you plant the right flowers and establish the right kind of shelter, wild guests of all kinds will move in.

Save the weeds Some weeds attract insects. Butterflies will suck nectar from the flowers. The peacock, the red admiral and the small tortoiseshell lay their eggs on nettles. When the eggs hatch out the caterpillars feed on the leaves.

Plant a hedge if you can. If you have one already, you will notice that it provides shelter and that birds like to feed and nest in it.

Many garden flowers are good for wildlife. The buddlea bush and the ice plant will attract butterflies from miles around.

Bee borage Perhaps you only have a window box or a small patch. You can grow bee borage.

1 Get a packet of borage seeds and sprinkle them on a layer of seed compost or clean soil laid out in a tray. Cover the seeds with a thin layer of compost or soil and water well.

2 Place the tray in a large polythene bag on a windowsill until the seeds have germinated. Water occasionally so the soil doesn't dry out.

3 When your seeds have sprouted into tiny seedlings, remove the polythene bag.

4 When the tiny borage plants have grown a few leaves you can transplant them into a windowbox, or a large plant pot for the patio, or directly into the soil in your conservation patch if the weather is warm.

Many butterflies as well as bees will visit your borage wherever it is.

A bundle of drinking straws held together with sticky tape can be pinned underneath a windowbox or windowsill. Small bees and wasps will nest inside. Brightly coloured straws will attract the insects.

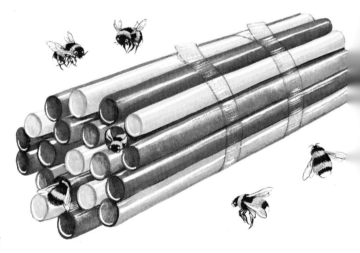

Leave a few large stones around for invertebrates to hide under. In many countries this is where scorpions rest during the heat of the day. It is also a popular woodlice retreat. How many kinds can you find?

Make a pile of logs This acts as a hotel for many small animals. If you build a really big pile you may attract a fox, even in a city. Out in the country, log piles left near streams may shelter mink and otters.

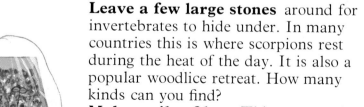

Water is important to all animals. If you provide some, many creatures will come to your conservation patch to drink.

● A bird bath can be made from an old meat tray. You'll get hours of fun watching the birds queuing up to bathe.

● Dig a pond, if there's room. A piece of heavy duty plastic will contain the water but be careful not to get holes in it. You can grow rushes and other waterplants round the edge. Bats and insect-eating birds like to feed near water in the evening. Many animals will come to drink and feed there.

Build a hedgehog house for hedgehogs to hibernate in.

1 Fill a wooden box with straw and cover it over with heavy plastic.

2 Make a hole in the side of the box and attach a large piece of pipe to it, to act as a tunnel. This will keep predators out.

3 Encourage hedgehogs by leaving a saucerful of milk out each night. You may also get other animals coming to feed.

POND DIPPING

Pond dipping is great fun and you always find something exciting. Take a net and some containers to put your finds in. You'll also need a hand lens to examine them. Don't forget your rubber boots. Tell an adult where you are going.

Creep up quietly to the stream or pond. There may be birds like herons fishing there already, or fish basking.

First of all, pass your net along the surface of the water. Here you'll find pondskaters and whirling beetles as well as mosquito larvae. There are flatworms up here as well as in the mud. Now swish the net through the water weeds. This is where the snails live. Lastly, check out the bottom. Here you will find caddis fly larvae and tubifex worms too.

You can take your finds home to keep in a bucket for a few days, but the best idea is to set up a proper aquarium. Take home a large container of water rich in microscopic life.

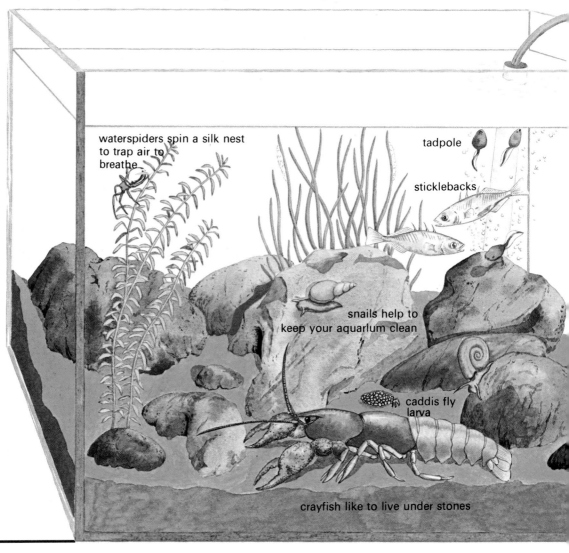

waterspiders spin a silk nest to trap air to breathe

tadpole

sticklebacks

snails help to keep your aquarlum clean

caddis fly larva

crayfish like to live under stones

SETTING UP A FRESHWATER AQUARIUM

1 A glass aquarium can be bought from a petshop, together with the various accessories you need to make the filtration system work.

2 Put the aquarium on a solid table. When it is full of water it will be very heavy and difficult to move. Don't put it on a windowsill or in direct sunlight.

3 It is not necessary to use a filter at all if you are prepared to change the water every few days. But if you want to keep your aquatic creatures for a long time, then a filter is the best way to keep the water clean and the animals healthy.

4 At the bottom of the aquarium place your plastic undergravel filter. Attach the filter tube at one end, placing it towards the back of the tank so that it can be hidden by rocks and weed. Attach a length of airpipe to your airstone and lower it down the pipe. Then attach the other end of the airpipe to a 2-way gang valve which you attach to the side of the aquarium. A second airpipe is used to connect this valve to the electrically driven airpump.

5 You can sterilize the gravel properly by putting it in the oven in an old baking tin for half an hour at a reasonably high temperature. Let it cool before putting it in the aquarium.

6 Smooth the gravel over the filter, banking it up a bit towards the back. Then place some attractive rocks in the tank. This is not just decoration but shelter for the fish and something for them to graze over. Plant some weeds in the gravel. Then pour water gently into the aquarium.

7 Place a cover over the tank to keep out dust. Let the water settle for 24 hours before putting animals in.

Remember that many animals are carnivorous and may eat each other. Beware particularly of the great diving beetle which will eat prey many times its own size. If in doubt, keep your animal in a separate container for a few days until you work out its habits.

AQUARIUM STARS

Tiny creatures need to be looked at with a magnifying glass or hand lens. Put them in a shallow dish to get the best view. Or you could make *a viewing chamber*. Take two pieces of glass and place a rubber tube in a U shape between them. Now clip the glass together with two large bulldog clips. You can pour a little water into the U between the glass pieces and drop in the creature you want to examine.

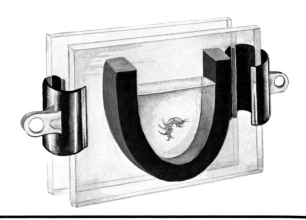

FROGS AND TOADS

Frogs and toads spend most of their life on land living in damp, overgrown places out of sight of enemies that might eat them, such as herons, storks and snakes. In Spring they return to breed in the ponds and ditches where they were born. The male and female cling together for many hours as the eggs are laid. You will probably hear them croaking.

KEEPING TADPOLES

1 Keep frog spawn and toad spawn separate, in different containers.
2 An aquarium, a large glass jar or a large ice cream container are all suitable for tadpoles. Cover with wire mesh.
3 Put the container near a window, but not in sunlight. Add some pond weed.

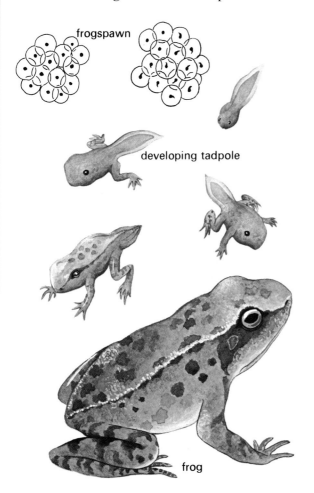

frogspawn

developing tadpole

frog

4 Tadpoles develop faster in warm conditions. It is interesting to compare the development of your tadpoles with those outside in the pond.
5 At first, each egg looks like a black dot. After a week it changes to a comma shape as the tadpole's head and tail appear. After ten days the tadpoles come out of the jelly surrounding them to rest on the weed nearby. If you look closely you will see that each has feathery gills through which it breathes oxygen from the water. After five weeks the gills drop off and the tadpole breathes like a fish. About this time the back legs appear. To begin with tadpoles eat algae or rasp at pondweed. They may like small pieces of lettuce.
6 When the front legs appear give the tadpoles a daily supply of pond water that is rich in microscopic life. Or you can suspend a small piece of meat in the water. Don't let the meat rot. If the water goes cloudy, change it straight away. You have got a pollution problem and your tadpoles are in danger.
7 Float a small piece of wood so the tadpoles can crawl out when they want to leave the water.
8 Now it's time to return the frogs to the wild. Put them in a damp place near the pond in which you found them. Or introduce them to a new pond. They may return to breed next year.

NEWTS

While you are pond dipping, you may come across *newts*. Like frogs and toads, they are only aquatic for part of the year. You can take one home to place in your aquarium for a few weeks. If you are collecting pond weed nearby, you may find not one newt but ten in your tank. This is because you have collected a waterplant laden with eggs. When the eggs hatch, perfectly formed little newts emerge. Baby newts have external gills.

THE VIVARIUM

You might like to keep your newts for a little while. In which case you should build a vivarium. This can house animals such as mice, voles and lizards.

A vivarium is basically a large empty fishtank filled with all the things that your animal likes best. So a vivarium for a newt would have a lot of green plants growing in soil, together with a shallow dish of water to create a pool. Keep it all very damp.

But maybe you want to keep scorpions? Your vivarium should then have a layer of sand at the bottom and be kept very dry.

Keeping animals in a vivarium:

newt

Eats: slugs, worms, insects, small invertebrates

Habitat: damp with a pool of water

slow-worm

Eats: slugs, snails, worms, insects

Habitat: slightly damp, needs stones to hide under

frog

Eats: small flies, beetles, slugs, worms

Habitat: damp. Needs pool of water

grass snake

Eats: tad-poles, frogs, toads, small mammals

Habitat: a warm place

toad

Eats: snails, young newts, frogs

Habitat: damp. Needs pool of water

mouse

Eats: wheat, grass, fruit, nuts

Habitat: compost with moss and turf. Straw for bedding

lizard

Eats: small insects – mealworms, blowflies

Habitat: sandy soil; needs a log to bask on

vole

Eats: grass, wheat, fruit, mealworms

Habitat: compost with moss and turf. Straw for bedding

FUNGI

Fungi are vital to life on earth because they recycle the nourishing parts from dying things. You see a lot of mushrooms and toadstools in autumn when the leaves drop off the trees and there is plenty for them to feed on. If you shake a toadstool on to a piece of white paper you will see powdery spores drop out. Each of these spores can turn into another fungus. Sometimes the wind spreads spores, and sometimes insects help.

The **stinkhorn fungus** is very smelly. It smells so bad you can track it down in an autumn wood by its odour alone. Flies are drawn to it to feed on its slime so, of course, they pick up spores as well. A single speck of fly excrement may contain millions of stinkhorn fungus spores. They can grow into new fungi. So why aren't there stinkhorn fungi everywhere? The reason must be that fungi are very choosy about the places they grow. There are all sorts of different fungi, pushing billions of spores into the air. Fortunately for us, only a few of these spores will land in a place where they can develop.

Fungi like the **edible mushroom** and the **puffball** prefer grassy meadows. Others, like the **fly agaric** (above), will only grow in birch woods, feeding on fallen leaves. The **Jew's Ear fungus** is rarely found anywhere but on the trunks of fallen elder trees. The **mildew** that you sometimes find creating a blue-grey "dusty" effect on rose leaves is a fungus. So are the "rots" that kill seedlings and eat away at ripe fruit. Green apples are more resistant to fungi because their skin is waxier, and the rainborne spores cannot penetrate it.

Not only do we eat certain types of mushroom, but we use yeasts, to ferment our wine and beer and to make our bread rise. Penicillin, which grows as a mould, is a fungus too. We also use moulds in cheese making.

HOW TO MAKE A SPORE PRINT

1 Cut the stalk from the cap and discard.
2 Place the cap on paper and cover it with a bowl for a few hours.
3 Remove cap and spray fixative on the spore print from above so the jet of air does not disturb the spores.

PRESERVE A FUNGI USING HOT SAND

Place your fungi in a tin tray then heat up a quantity of sand in the oven and pour it over your fungi. Use gloves so you don't get burnt. Leave to cool before removing.

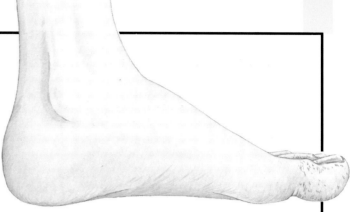

DIFFERENT MOULDS

1 Take an orange and a piece of bread.
2 Put them on different plates and place them in warm, moist places in your house. You could put one in the bathroom and another in the kitchen.
3 Do they grow the same mould?
4 If they grow different moulds, try the experiment again but swap the places round.

Some fungi grow on us. Athlete's foot is a sore that you often pick up in swimming pools. The fish in your aquarium may develop fungal diseases like fin rot. Whilst most of these fungal activities are just a nuisance, some of them can kill.

Changing the landscape The activities of fungi can change the landscape. Many serious tree diseases are caused by fungi. The English countryside looks very different today, compared with twenty years ago, because Dutch Elm Disease has killed more than 11 million trees. In North America oaks suffer from Oak Wilt and in Europe the beech is threatened by Beech Bark Disease. Insects spread the spores of the fungi and high winds also contribute.

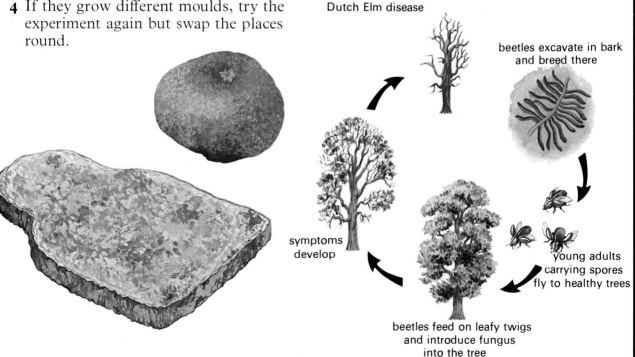

Dutch Elm disease

beetles excavate in bark and breed there

young adults carrying spores fly to healthy trees

beetles feed on leafy twigs and introduce fungus into the tree

symptoms develop

THE SEASHORE

At the seashore, what you do depends on whether the tide is in or out. It's just the same for the animals that live there. Underwater a limpet is able to move around the rock grazing on algae. When the tide goes out it must withdraw into its shell and stick hard to the rockface to protect itself from battering waves, hot sunshine and hungry birds.

Find out what a limpet does underwater by marking its shell and the spot you found it in, with nail varnish. At low tide move it to another rock. Next day you will find it has returned to its first home.

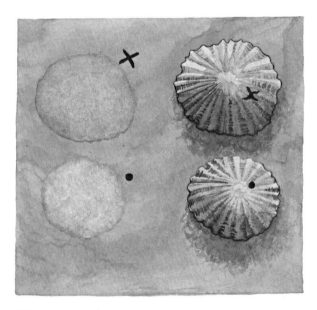

Watch underwater creatures through a diving mask. You can lie on the rocks with your head in the water of a rockpool. Or you can take a look at the seabed.

MAKE A VIEWING BOX TO SEE UNDERWATER

1 Take a large plastic box or bowl and cut a hole in the bottom. Leave a lip.
2 Now glue a piece of glass or perspex over the hole. Use a strong glue or silicon cement. Cling film will do if you carry it right up over the sides of the box and secure it at the top.
3 Now you can use your box to see underwater without getting wet.

FISHWATCH

Fish often get stranded in rock pools. If you wear polaroid sunglasses to cut out reflected light and sit very quietly you can easily study them. You may see young flatfish if you move a stick vigorously in a sandy pool. These fish (dabs, flounders, plaice and sole) breed just offshore. To begin with, a flatfish isn't flat, and it has eyes on both sides of its head. But as it adopts a bottom dwelling life, its eyes gradually move to the top.

DANGER FISH

If you live in the tropics you should always wear shoes when searching rock pools. There are several marine organisms that could severely hurt you. Stonefish and certain jellyfish can be dangerous. Check with an adult who knows the area and its wildlife well.

SEAWEEDS

Seaweeds are marine algae. Each type of seaweed is particular to a certain part of the shore. Here are a few common ones.

At the top of the beach grow the green **sea lettuce**, **grass kelp** and **sea moss.**

In the middle zone you usually find brown seaweeds. **Channelled wrack** is the first of these. It rolls up its fronds to prevent itself from drying out. You will also find **flat wracks** and on rough, exposed beaches masses of **bladder wrack.**

Lower down, in deep, dark pools you will notice various types of red seaweed. **Red laver** is good to eat.

SEAWEED PRESSING

You can press seaweeds to make a collection, rather like you press flowers.

1 Arrange the seaweed in a bowl of water.
2 Slide white paper under it and lift it all out on to a pile of newspapers.
3 Cover with muslin and another layer of newspapers. Place a book on top. Not a heavy weight or the seaweed will get stuck to the newspaper.
4 While the seaweed is wet, change the newspaper every day.

EBB AND FLOW

The moon influences the tides. Twice a month – when the moon is full and when it is new – there are big tides. More of the beach is exposed at low tide on these days. It is then that you will find kelps and thongweeds growing on the rocks. If you look amongst the Holdfasts, which are the discs or rootlike branches that attach the seaweed to the rocks, you will find mussels, sea urchins and swimming crabs.

Do watch out when exploring an isolated shoreline that you don't get cut off by the incoming sea. It's very easy to forget the time when there are lots of fascinating items to collect.

KEEPING MARINE ANIMALS

The animals you find in a rockpool are adaptable. You can take some of them home in a bucket to watch at night when they are most active. If you change the water for fresh seawater every day, you can keep your animals alive for some time. Watch out for milky traces in the water which indicate pollution.

A TEMPORARY AQUARIUM
It is very expensive to install a permanent marine aquarium but a temporary one is easy to set up.
1 Prepare the aquarium before you go collecting. Get a plastic or glass tank with no metal parts that will rust.
2 Spread a layer of sand in the bottom then add a few rocks with all traces of seaweed scrubbed off.
3 If you have no filtration system you *must* change the water for fresh seawater every day. Siphon it out.

SUITABLE GUESTS
● Rocks that are encrusted with **mussels, acorn barnacles** and **tube worms** are good to watch at night.
● **Prawns** and **shrimps** are very active.
● **Anemones**. They look like plants but are really animals. Put two close together and they will fight – very slowly.
● **Brittle stars** and **starfish**.
● **Crabs** are great – but they eat everything else!
● **Mussels** filter the water clean.
  DON'T put in any seaweed. It will rot.
  Sponges, **limpets** and **seaslugs** do not thrive.
  Try to return all your animals when you have finished watching them.

SEA SHELLS
The seashells you find along the beach are the abandoned homes of molluscs. Some shells are in two parts, hinged together.

They are called bivalves. *Mussels* and *oysters* are bivalves. Most of these animals live in the sand. They emerge when the tide is high to suck water through their bodies, using siphon tubes. The other type of shell is in the form of a spiral, like a land snail. You can file the side of an empty shell so that you can see inside.

It's interesting to collect shells from the tideline, but don't buy shells from shops. These have been caught in deep water and the animal killed for its shell.

SEASHORE COLLECTION

A seashore collection card is an attractive way to display any interesting things you have found at the seaside. A darkish colour card will show off your shells, seaweeds, rocks and fossils perfectly.

Above: some common shells found on many beaches.

Some cone shells found in tropical waters are poisonous and dangerous to man. Make sure you only collect empty shells from the seashore.

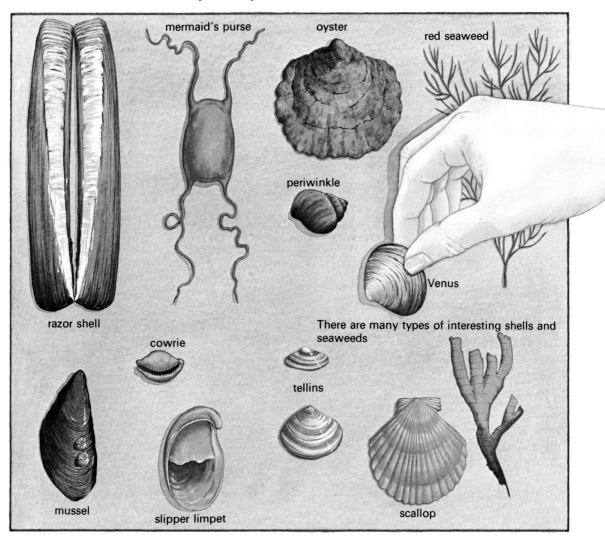

mermaid's purse

oyster

red seaweed

periwinkle

Venus

razor shell

There are many types of interesting shells and seaweeds

cowrie

tellins

mussel

slipper limpet

scallop

BIRDWATCHING

There are just over 9,000 species of birds in the world. South America has the most with 2,500 types. Birds are all around us, even in cities. There are so many, and they always seem to fly away before you get a good look at them. How can you learn about birds?

Binoculars Investing in a good pair of binoculars is a wise move. If you have a choice, 8 × 30 or 8 × 40 magnification are the sort to buy.

Next step Give yourself a head start by finding out the names of the birds that live and visit the area in which you are birdwatching. Each locality (seashore, mountain, marshland, garden) has its own birds which vary with the season. Local birdwatchers can help you. You can learn from books too. Best of all, join a club (like the Royal Society for the Protection of Birds in Great Britain) and go bird-watching with some real experts.

What to look out for Each species has its own identification characteristics. A distinctive tail shape perhaps. Or you may notice the hooked beak of a bird of prey. Often birds' special flight pattern tells you what they are. Do they fly straight or in an undulating way?

When a bird rises up in front of you, try to work out its size. Is it bigger than a sparrow? Smaller than a swan? What is the call like? Are there any bars on the wings or tail? As you become more ex-perienced, all these questions will flash through your mind – and be answered – almost instantaneously. You will know at once what the bird is. This is called getting the "jizz" of the bird.

Bird pellets Many birds of prey, owls in particular, cough up pellets of the in-digestible parts of their prey. So if you look in barns and derelict buildings where owls roost, you will find these cylindrical parcels of compacted fur, bone and feath-ers on the floor.

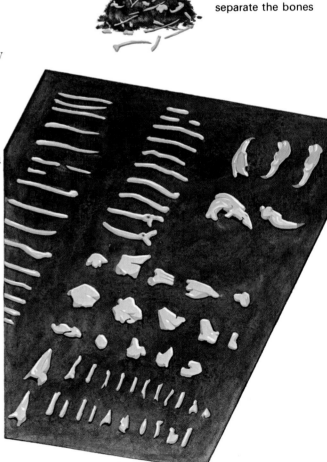

soak pellet in water

separate the bones

DISSECT THE PELLET TO FIND OUT WHAT THE OWL HAS BEEN EATING

1 Drop the pellet in a jar of water. Put a top on it.
2 Shake the jar gently every few hours to swill away fur and feathers.
3 Pour away the debris and lay the bones on a sheet of white paper to identify.
4 If you want to make a collection you should bleach the bones in hydrogen peroxide. Lay them out in neat groups on a black card according to type.

MAKING A HIDE

1 Make a wooden frame. Poles, firmly planted in the ground and secured at the corners with cord are sufficient.
2 Cover it with greenish brown cotton, canvas or sacking. Heavy stones will prevent the material flapping.
3 Cut peepholes and tack some black netting securely behind them.
4 Let the birds get used to the hide for a few days before you use it. Then get a friend to accompany you in and out of the hide. When your friend walks away, leaving you in the hide, the birds will think you have both gone.

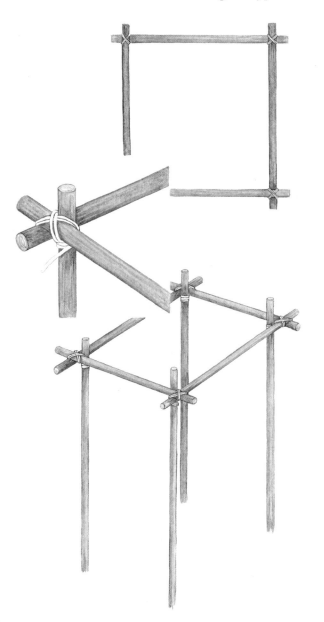

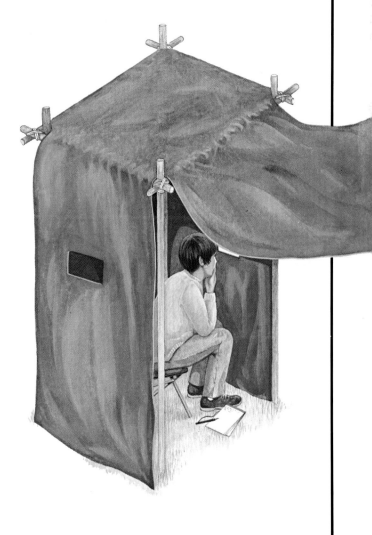

BUILDING FOR BIRDS

Many birds migrate in the autumn to avoid cold weather. You can help the ones that stay behind by putting food out on a bird table every day. This will save many lives. Scraps of bread and cake are always eaten. Tits like a container full of peanuts and you will enjoy watching them swinging around on an upturned coconut. In cold weather, pieces of fat are very good for birds. Remember to stop feeding them when spring arrives and they start breeding. They need natural food at this time.

A SIMPLE BIRD TABLE
You will need: a flat piece of wood ● 4 battens ● nails and hammer ● 1 post

Nail battens and post to the flat wood as in the diagram. Dig post into the ground. Make sure it is steady. Attach fat etc.

MAKE A COLLECTION OF FEATHERS
Feathers are what makes a bird different from all other animals. After all, there are many creatures that sing or call, lay eggs or migrate. Bats (which are mammals) fly too. But only birds have feathers.

Feathers probably evolved from reptilian scales millions of years ago. Today birds use them to attract a mate, and to warm their eggs as well as to fly with.

Mount your feathers on card. Attach them by a small staple across the shaft.

TROPICAL DRINK

If you live in the tropics you can attract nectar-eating birds like humming birds and sunbirds to your garden by putting out inverted bottles full of sugar and water.

MAKING A NEST BOX

You will need: wood 15 cm wide (6 in) and 18 cm ($\frac{3}{4}$ in) thick • saw • nails • hammer • glue • wood preservative • hinge • catch

Increase the number of birds breeding in your garden or your conservation patch. A nest box can be bought from garden centres or you can make one yourself.

1 Cut up wood to sizes in diagram. The hole should be 29 mm ($1\frac{1}{8}$ in) across.
2 Nail, screw or glue pieces together as in diagram.
3 Treat with non-smelly wood preservative.
4 Attach hinge to lid and attach simple catch to front.

top | side | side | back | front | floor

5 Nail on tree out of reach of cats and other predators. It should be placed on the sheltered side of the tree.
Robins sometimes nest in odd containers left in the hedge.

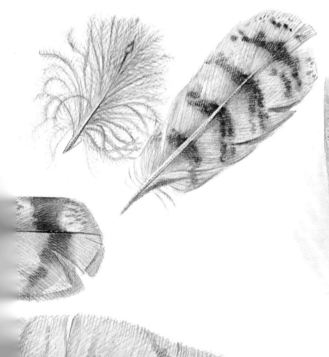

Nestboxes are very important for some rare birds. In Britain, the pied flycatcher is an uncommon bird, but its population is growing since ornithologists found that it prefers nestboxes to holes in trees.

...RGE SWEEP NET

...a piece of wire or a metal coat-hanger and twist it into a circle. Twist the loose ends together and attach them to a stick with a second piece of wire.

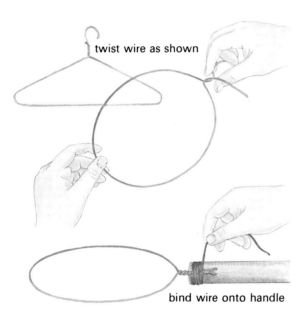

twist wire as shown

bind wire onto handle

thread net onto frame

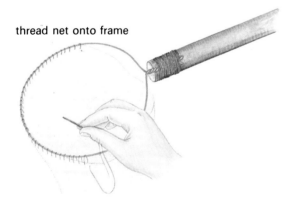

2 Make a cotton bag and attach this to the wire.

3 In an area of long grass, gently sweep the net to and fro. You should find many insects including caterpillars and pupae of various butterflies and moths.

4 Turn these out on to a white dish or cloth to examine.

Butterflies and moths have four stages in their lives. This is because an insect's skeleton is outside its body. It is a tough case of chiton. This protects the adult insect but does not allow it to grow. So in the early stage of its life as a caterpillar it is able to shed its skin from time to time.

KEEPING CATERPILLARS

1 You can keep caterpillars in a plastic box. An ice cream container is ideal.

2 Prick a few small holes in the top and place paper in the bottom. This will keep the humidity right.

3 Your caterpillar will need daily fresh food and a clean cage. Give it leaves from the plant on which you found it.

4 Now you can watch your caterpillar grow. It will split its skin several times and turn into a pupa (chrysalis). Put a twig in the box for it to hang from.

5 The pupa does not feed. During this period the insect is reorganizing all its cells into the shape of the adult insect. It often does this during the winter months so keep your box cool.

6 At last the adult insect emerges. It will want to feed on nectar, so you should release it near flowers.

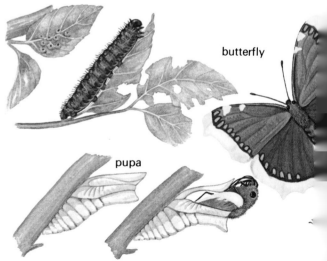

butterfly

pupa

CATCHING MOTHS WITH A LIGHT TRAP AT NIGHT

1 Tie a sheet from some branches of a tree during a period of warm weather.

2 Set up a bright electric torch so that the beam falls on the white fabric.

3 Many insects will be drawn to the light. Catch and examine them in a wide jar.

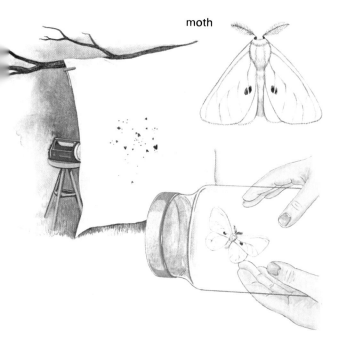

moth

You can keep some of your finds under a **gauze meat cover** placed on a wide tray. This is normally used for keeping insects out, but it is also excellent for keeping them in.

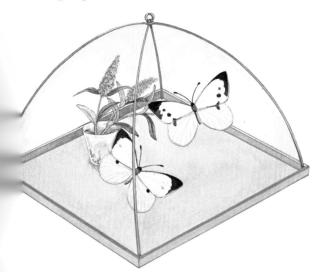

MAKE A POOTER

You will need: a length of pipe ● 2 rubber bungs with holes through them ● a glass tube.

Many insects are too small to handle easily, and a pooter will enable you to pick them up without hurting them.

1 Cut the pipe into two short lengths. Push them through the bungs and put the bungs into each end of the tube.

2 Now you can suck up the insect into the tube to transfer it from one place to another.

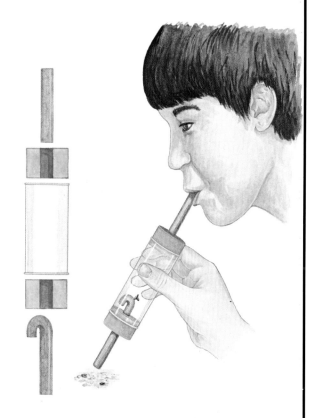

Use your pooter to collect ladybirds Ladybirds are fun to keep and you can get them to lay eggs if you keep their cage absolutely clean and give them plenty of their favourite food, the aphid. Both adults and grubs eat a lot of aphids every day. The grubs will pupate for a week before turning into adult ladybirds.

...rees in the world are the giant ...is in California which can reach ...o 111.25 m (365 ft) in height. Some Californian redwoods are reckoned to be over four thousand years old.

HOW TO MEASURE THE HEIGHT OF A TREE

(You need a friend to help.)

1 Hold a pencil in front of you at arm's length, so that the bottom of the pencil is level with the base of the tree and the top of the pencil coincides with the crown of the tree.
2 Now turn the pencil sideways, keeping the base of it in line with the bottom of the tree.

BARK RUBBING

1 Take a sheet of strong paper and tie or pin it to a tree.
2 Now rub the surface all over with cobbler's heel ball or a thick wax crayon.
3 You will get some great effects which you can vary by using different coloured paper or wax. You can mount some of your best ones on stiff card.

Bark protects trees from damage and disease. Each species of tree has a different bark pattern.

3 Ask your friend to walk away from the tree until he or she reaches the point that corresponds with the end of your pencil.
4 If you measure the distance between your friend and the tree, that should equal its height.

GROW YOUR OWN OAK TREE

It's easy to grow your own tree. Trees flower and, with the help of insects to pollinate them, they set seed like other plants. You have probably found sprouting seeds like acorns in the autumn.

1 Take a large plant pot and put a few pieces of broken flower pot in the bottom for drainage.
2 Fill the pot three-quarters full of potting compost or clean soil, with no weeds.
3 Place your acorn in the pot and cover it over with more soil.
4 Water the pot well and place it in a sheltered place. It should send up shoots quite quickly. Make sure the pot does not dry out. Water regularly.
5 Your tree will not need much attention until it grows out of its pot. Then you must find a permanent place for it. Somewhere, hopefully, that you can return to look at it year after year and watch it grow to maturity. Protect your tree with some wire-netting held in place by four stakes. Many animals, like rabbits and sheep browse on young trees.

Note: Acorn and horse-chestnut seeds germinate quickly. Other seeds often take a few months to get going.

BUDS

In the spring you can take some buds into the warmth of your house to watch the leaves uncurl. As the bud grows the scales are pushed apart and the leaves uncurl. The new leaves are pale but as they start to use the sunlight, the carbon dioxide in the air and water-borne nutrients, they deepen in colour.

HOW CAN YOU TELL THE AGE OF A TREE

1 If you run a tape measure round the trunk of a mature tree you will get a rough idea because the age of a tree often corresponds to the circumference in inches (1 in is 2.5 cm). Therefore a tree 24 in is about 24 years old.
2 A more accurate method is to count the annual rings in a cross section of the tree trunk. Trees form new layers of water-carrying tissue under the bark each year. If you can find a tree stump or a fallen tree, you can count them.

Leaf rubbing

Place leaf (not too dry) on a flat surface

Cover with tissue and hold firmly

Rub with soft pencil or crayon

MAMMALS

Mammals are animals which suckle their young. Many mammals will be very familiar to you either because you see them every day like dogs, horses, cats and sheep, or because you have seen them in wildlife programmes on television or in safari parks or zoos, like lions, tigers, elephants, giraffes and so on.

But some mammals are very shy and there are many mammals living near you that you will seldom see, such as mice and voles.

Some mammals are nocturnal, that is they only appear at night and sleep during the day. If you are very careful, still and quiet, it is sometimes possible to see a nocturnal mammal like a badger or a hedgehog or more often a fox.

Sometimes you can see which animals have passed by, by indentifying their footprints in snow or mud. There are other ways, too, of knowing when a mammal is around.

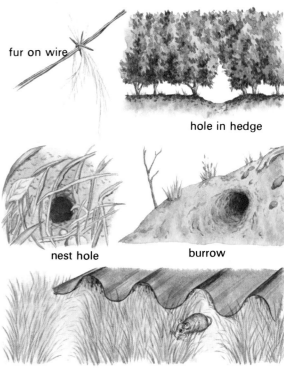

fur on wire

hole in hedge

nest hole

burrow

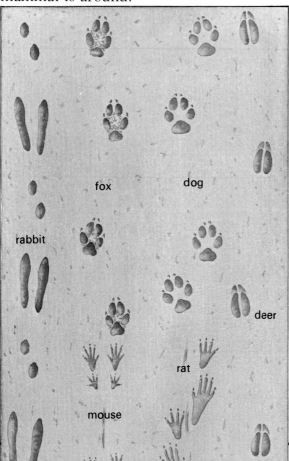

fox

dog

rabbit

deer

rat

mouse

If you take an old sheet of corrugated iron and leave it flat on the soil for a few months you will find that many animals will set up home underneath it. Watch out in countries where there are poisonous snakes though! That's just the kind of place they like to hide.

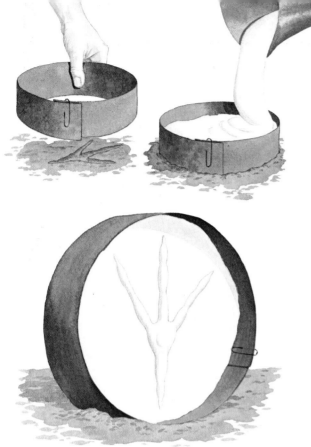

RECONSTRUCTING A SKELETON

It's a real challenge to reconstruct a skeleton! You may find a dead rabbit or you could try a mouse.

1 Attach string to its leg and bury it, so that one end of the string is visible and you can find the burial place again.
2 Leave for several weeks until there is no flesh left on the bones.
3 Dig up the skeleton with great care, gently brushing debris from the bones.
4 Carefully glue the bones together or attach with thin wire. Try to find a picture of the skeleton to guide you.

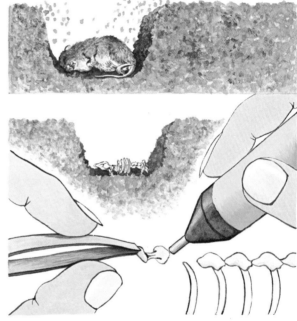

MAKING A PLASTER CAST

You will need: cardboard strip 30 cm (11¾ in) × 5 cm (2 in) ● paper clips ● trowel ● plastic bowl ● spoon ● newspapers.

Along the bed of a shallow stream there are muddy places where birds and animals have left tracks. Try to to make a plaster cast of some.

1 Clip your cardboard into a circle and place it over the track into the mud.
2 Mix plaster of Paris with clean stream-water and pour the mixture into the mould.
3 Plaster of Paris sets very quickly. You should be able to dig up the plaster cast after about fifteen minutes. Leave the cardboard round it. Wrap it all up in newspaper before carrying it.

VARIETY IS THE SPICE OF LIFE

There are so many different mammals it is hard to believe they have anything in common. Here are a few of them.

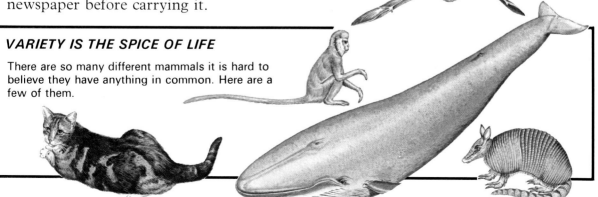

PLANTS

Plants have many strategies for spreading their seeds. Some are carried on the wind and others by animals. You can find out just how many seeds are lying about in the soil by digging up a clod of earth early in the year, just before the growing season starts. Put it in a shallow tin or seed box, place it on a windowsill and water it regularly. You'll be amazed at how much life that soil contains.

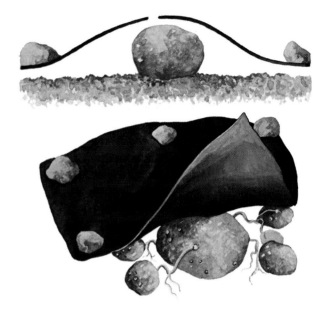

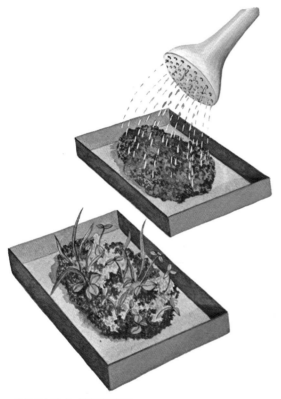

GROW A POTATO

Not all plants reproduce by spreading seeds. Some grow new plants from special rootlike stems (rhizomes) that spread underground.

You can watch this process by clearing a small patch of ground and planting a potato. Don't plant it in the usual way. Just put it on the top of the soil and cover it with dense, black polythene 1 m (39 in) square covers one potato). Make a little hole just over the potato for the stem to grow through. To see how your potato is growing just pull back the polythene.

GERMINATE A BEAN

1 Soak a couple of beans in water overnight.
2 Put them in a jar lined with moist blotting paper. Put water at the bottom.
3 Place the beans somewhere warm, but not in full sun. Don't let them dry out.
4 It doesn't matter which way up the beans are. The roots and shoots are sensitive to gravity. They know which is the right way to grow. Try confusing them by turning them round.

PRESSING FLOWERS

Arrange your flower carefully on absorbent paper (such as blotting paper) and cover it with a further layer of paper. Place the plant between two boards and weight it down with a heavy pile of books. (You can buy special flower presses.) The flower will dry out in a few days. You can then mount it in a folder. It's a good idea to make notes of where you picked it and the time of year you found it flowering.

Seed dispersal

Many seeds are dispersed by the wind

You can disperse some seeds yourself

Some seeds are barbed and are carried by animals in their coats and on their paws

Some seeds are dispersed by birds on their beaks and claws

PLANTS

If it were not for plants man could not exist. They provide us with oxygen to breathe and with food.

GERMINATE CRESS ON A WINDOWSILL
1 Soak your cress seeds overnight in a dish of water.
2 Put some layers of tissue or paper in a margarine tub.
3 Dampen the paper and spread the seeds over it.
4 Put the tub on a windowsill and watch the seeds grow. Water them well.
5 Make a sandwich and eat your crop.

WATCH PLANTS PUMP WATER
1 Take a white flower and place it in a pot of water dyed with cake colouring. The petals soon change colour.
2 Split the stem and put one half in coloured water and the other half in plain or another colour. Watch the water rise.

3 If you cut a slice across the stem you can see the bundles of vessels that carry water and sap up the plant.

FLOWER POWER

It is fascinating to collect flowers, but don't take big bunches. Many wild flowers are getting rare. Some of them are protected by law.

PLANT PHOTOGRAPHY

Dead flowers always lose their colour. But photographs preserve the detail of the plant and its habitat.

You will need a camera with a lens that can focus on objects that are placed close-up in front of it. Many standard lenses on modern 35 mm cameras are described as "macro" and are perfect for the job. A small tripod is useful but you can make a special spike for plant photography by welding a ball and socket head with a camera fitting on to a metal rod.

Ideally, you should always do plant photography on brightly lit, windless days. Unfortunately, it doesn't take much of a breeze to make a flowerhead shiver, so it's a good idea to make a windbreak to protect your subject. If you make it out of white material it will also act as a light reflector.

Note the names of the flowers you have photographed so you don't get muddled.

DRAWING AND PAINTING FLOWERS

Get a basic understanding of the shape of the flower. Dissect one to see how the petals and stamens lie. You can use pencils, crayons or watercolours. Fine Edding or Rotring pens with coloured inks laid on with a fine brush have a very attractive effect.

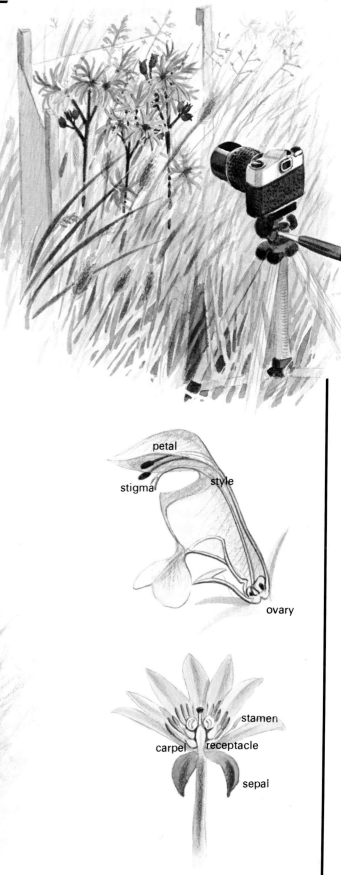

petal

stigma

style

ovary

stamen

carpel

receptacle

sepal

THE SOIL

If you dig down through the soil you will notice several layers. At the top is the leaf litter. This is rich in dying plant material and here you find many different kinds of mites feeding. Ants and spiders hunt here. As you turn the soil over you may find the pupae of moths and other insects. It is interesting to look under stones. Sometimes you find frogs, toads and newts buried in their chamber homes. Small mammals like voles and shrews make nests in the earth.

MAKE A WORMERY

You will need: 2 pieces of perspex ● 3 pieces of wood ● screws

1 Collect the worms. Banging a fork, stuck in the ground, will attract worms.
2 Fill the wormery with layers of different soils. You could put a layer of washed sand or gravel, mud from a stream, lighter soil from a hilltop.
3 Place a layer of leaves on top. Then install the worms. If you keep the wormery dark and moist the worms will be very comfortable.

Did you know that there are thousands of different sorts of worms? Many of them live in the soil, but others live in ponds, ditches and streams. Many live in the sea. The biggest earthworm comes from Australia and is over 3 m ($3\frac{1}{4}$ yd) long. There are over three thousand different types of earthworm. If you walk across a lawn on a warm, damp night you will find earthworms coming to the surface to look for food or to mate. Earthworms are hermaphrodites which means they are

If a perspex wormery is too expensive, you can use a jam jar. Fill it with layers of different soils and place leaves on top. Wrap dark paper around the jar, so that the worms will come to the sides.

Remember to keep the wormery dark and moist.

SOIL LAYER JAR

You will need: a milk bottle or jar • a plastic funnel • cotton wool • a jam jar • sand • clay • water • soil.

1 Place about 4 cm (1½ in) of soil in a jar or milk bottle.
2 Fill three-quarters full of water. Shake vigorously.
3 Leave to settle. Soil will have separated into distinct layers. The heaviest particles will be on the bottom and the lightest ones nearest the top.

1 Dig a hole in the soil to fit your tin or jar.
2 Place the bricks on either side of the hole with the wood over the top.
3 Place some food at the bottom of the jar to attract small animals.
4 When you have caught something, pick up the whole container and empty it into a cotton bag, if you are taking your animal home.
5 The best place to keep small mammals is a purpose made box with plenty of ventilation. However, for a short time you could use a vivarium like the one on page 9 that is converted from an old aquarium.
6 When you have finished watching your animal, release it in the place you caught it, so it can go home.

both male and female. When they have mated with each other, both worms will make a cocoon full of eggs which they will leave to develop in the soil. After a few weeks one or two fully formed young worms will hatch out.

Worms are very good for the soil because they aerate it with their burrows. Their digging mixes the upper humus layers of the soil which are rich in fallen leaves and nutrients, with the poorer, stonier subsoil beneath.

A PITFALL TRAP

You will need: a large, deep tin or jar with smooth sides • four bricks • large piece of wood.

This can be very successful in catching small animals of all kinds.

HUNGRY FUNGI

Some fungi eat tiny animals in the soil. They are able to capture amoeba, which get stuck on sticky parts of the thread-like underground hypha. Some fungi produce a substance that sets like instant glue when microscopic worms or mites pass by. Fungi even set traps for their prey.

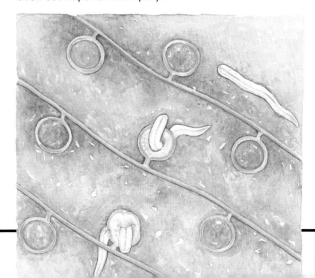

Index

Acorns, to grow, 23
Aquarium, 2, 6, 9
   freshwater, to make, 7–8
   seawater, to make, 14

Bark rubbing, 22
Beans, to grow, 26
Bee borage, to grow, 4
Binoculars, 3, 16
Birds, 4, 16–19
   bird bath, to make, 5
   bird pellets, 16–17
   bird table, to make, 18
Bones, 2, 17, 25
Buds, leaf, 23
Butterflies, 4, 20

Caterpillars, 2, 4, 20
Cress, to grow, 28

Feathers, 18
Fish, 12, 14
Fishing net, 3, 6
Flowers, 4
   flower drawing, 29
   flower pressing, 27
Footprints, 24–5
Fox, 24
Frog, 8–9, 30
Fungi, 10–11, 31

Grass snake, 9

Hand lens, 3, 6–7
Hedge, 4
Hedgehog, 5, 24
Hides, to make, 3, 17

Insects, 4, 20–1

Ladybird, 21
Limpet, 12
Lizard, 9

Magnifying glass, 3, 6–7
Moth, 20–1, 30
Mould, 10–11
Mouse, 9
Mushroom, 10

Nature diary, 2
Nature table, 2
Nest box, to make, 19
Nets
   fishing, to make, 3, 6
   sweep, to make, 20
Newt, 8–9, 30
Notebook, 2

Pellets, bird, 16–17
Photography, plant, 29
Plaster casts, to make, 25
Ponds, 3, 5–6, 8
Pooter, to make, 21
Potato, to grow, 26

Scorpion, 4, 9
Seaweed, 2, 13

Seeds, 4, 26–7
Shells, 2, 14–15
Skeleton, 25
Slow worm, 9
Snail, 5–6, 15
Snake, 8–9, 24
Spawn, frog/toad, 8
Spores, fungi, 10

Tadpoles, to keep, 8
Tides, 12–13
Toad, 8–9, 30
Toadstool, 10
Traps, to make
   light, 21
   pitfall, 31
Trees
   to age, 23
   to grow, 23
   to measure, 22

Viewing box, to make, 12
Viewing chamber, to make, 7
Vivarium, 9, 31
Vole, 9, 30

Weeds, 4
Worm, 30–1
   earth, 30–1
   flat, 6
   slow, 9
   tube, 14
   tubifex, 6
Wormery, to make, 31

Published in 1988 by
The Hamlyn Publishing Group Limited
a division of Paul Hamlyn Publishing
Michelin House, 81 Fulham Road, London SW3 6RB

Copyright © The Hamlyn Publishing Group Limited 1988

ISBN 0 600 55539 9

Printed and bound in Italy
Front jacket illustration: Heather Angel, Anwar Islam, Kenneth Oliver
Illustrations: Linden Artists (Jane Pickering, Michelle Ross, David Webb)
Simon Burr, John Michael Davis
Photographic acknowledgments: Liz and Tony Bomford, Peter Loughran, Hamlyn
Group Picture Library
Design: Tony Truscott
General editors: Gillian Denton, Lynne Williams